T0128726

A-Z
WAYS TO ACHIEVE
YOUR GOALS IN LIFE

Arinola O. Olawusi

authorHOUSE®

AuthorHouse™
1663 Liberty Drive
Bloomington, IN 47403
www.authorhouse.com
Phone: 1 (800) 839-8640

Published by AuthorHouse 04/21/2016

ISBN: 978-1-5246-0343-4 (sc)
ISBN: 978-1-5246-0342-7 (e)

Library of Congress Control Number: 2016906077

Print information available on the last page.

Any people depicted in stock imagery provided by Thinkstock are models, and such images are being used for illustrative purposes only. Certain stock imagery © Thinkstock.

This book is printed on acid-free paper.

Because of the dynamic nature of the Internet, any web addresses or links contained in this book may have changed since publication and may no longer be valid. The views expressed in this work are solely those of the author and do not necessarily reflect the views of the publisher, and the publisher hereby disclaims any responsibility for them.

KJV
Scripture quotations marked KJV are from the Holy Bible, King James Version (Authorized Version). First published in 1611. Quoted from the KJV Classic Reference Bible, Copyright © 1983 by The Zondervan Corporation.

NKJV
Scripture quotations marked NKJV are taken from the New King James Version. Copyright © 1982 by Thomas Nelson, Inc. Used by permission. All rights reserved.

Simple steps to reach your goals in this life.

This book is dedicated to the love of my life Olalekan Abinbola. Thank you for having so much belief in me.

CONTENTS

Always believe that you will succeed.............................1

Be determined..3

Create time for yourself...5

Don't Procrastinate..7

Envision yourself achieving your dream. 9

Focus on your goal. 11

Giving up is not an option 13

Have faith or belief in the Lord 15

If there is no pain, there is no gain. 17

Just keep moving yourself forward.............................19

K- Keep Benefitting Associations...............................21

Learn to Love yourself..23

Make good choices..25

Never forget to Plan ahead. 27

Organize your life 29

Preparing well pays off. 31

Quash all timewasters. 33

Read and Study, no matter what.................................35

Stay motivated..37

THINK BIG..39

Ultimately, YOU are the determinant of your future. . 41

Verbal out what want to become. 43

Wisdom is a virtue you should possess........................45

Xamine Yourself often..47

You are the one that determines your own luck. 49

Zeal is important..51

Always believe that you will succeed.

Think and believe and see yourself as success. You have got to believe that whatever goal you set to do will become a success. Do not think yourself as a cannot do, see yourself as a can do it. You can do it. Believe that anything you set your mind, soul and strength will be a success. Always see yourself on top of situations, making things happening, seeing things happen, acting out things to happen. See yourself as a possibility. The Holy Book says in Mark 9:23 (NKJV) paraphrase Jesus said to him "If you can believe, all things are possible to him who believes." It is not good for you to have a negative mentality, do have a positive (believing) mentality. If a glass is half filled with water, what do you see, you do see it as half filled (almost filled) or half empty (almost empty). Believe and see yourself succeeding and my dear you shall surely succeed. May the Lord bless you.

Action point: Are you embarking on a goal, an examination or a project. Deep down in your heart, believe that it will become a success. Picture yourself using your mind to see yourself succeeding in that examination, goal, journey or project. Do not have the mind that you will fail or that the goal will not succeed or that you will not have a safe journey or a successful project.

Let your mind eye see success in that endeavour by taking the timeout to see you succeeding. In the Holy Bible, the Lord had to take Abraham out in the night to count the number of stars so that he could picture his seeds being numerous_Genesis 15:5 (paraphrase). That is what you have to see yourself doing, with your inner or mind eye.

Be determined

Set your mind, soul and strength to that goal and project. Be a determiner that you will get there and you will, that you will achieve and you will. Ask the Holy Spirit to help you to be determined and he will, you need to be determined in the Holy Spirit because with human or carnal power, nothing can be achieved. We all need to constantly ask for the help of the Holy Spirit. The Bible says in Zechariah 4:6 "Not by might, not by power, but by my spirit, saith the Lord of hosts".

Show me a determined heart through the help of the Holy Spirit for a particular goal and I will show you a heart that can get that goal done. It is only with the help of the Holy Spirit.

Action Point: What is that thing you want to try to achieve, is it a certificate program, learning a skill, to read that book, sit down with yourself, close your eyes and determine within you that you will accomplish it. Now ask for the help of the Holy Spirit after you have prayed to help you through what you have just prayed for. Ask with the mind that you prayers are being heard by the Lord.

Create time for yourself

This is an act of being alone by oneself or being alone just with you and you alone. It helps you to think and find value from within. Do not focus too much on unimportant activities forgetting to spend adequate time with yourself. Some people spend their time, talking, being busy, chatting, welcoming others, except with themselves, thus they are always famished and weary. Sometimes in this life, you really have to focus from every other thing and focus on yourself alone. You will be able to determine your strengths, weaknesses and areas you need to work on in the different areas of your life. There is great wisdom derived from being alone. The Bible says in "Genesis 24:63 that Isaac went out into the field to meditate in the evening. He was creating time for himself, focusing on himself, being with himself by being alone. I tell you, it brings insight, joy, and ability to discover oneself. Learn to withdraw. Also in Luke 5:16. Jesus usually withdrew himself to a solitary place. I see you becoming a better person even as you withdraw and spend quality time with yourself.

Action Point: Select at least two days in a week, possibly at the beginning of the week or at the end of the week and locate one quiet and solitary area along with your pen and diary, stay quiet in that place. Then start to ask yourself questions like where am I spiritually, relationally, intellectually and professionally, ask yourself where you want to be in 3 months, 6 months and 9 months and 12 months (a year) from where you are. Dream, set goals and plans to achieve them. Draw a daily plan for yourself to achieve that goal. Have a dream, set weekly or daily goals, now, plan to achieve them and you will definitely become a Success.

Don't Procrastinate.

What is Procrastination? In simple words, it is postponing or putting till tomorrow what you can do today. It is being your own time-waster. It is caused by laziness or not wanting to do anything. If you want to become a force in this life, you definitely will not be postponing or putting till tomorrow that which you can do today. Some people postpone everything. They post pone going back to school, using their talents of gifts, even learning a skill. They say within their hearts "I will do it later". This is not a helpful phrase. Don't waste your time darling postponing till tomorrow what you can do today, something else could come up tomorrow which could eventually delay you from getting it done tomorrow and at the end, nothing gets done. Why can't you do it now, what are you doing that you can't do it now. Start it now. Start learning that skill. Take that class, learn that language, and go get that training. Don't procrastinate. When you do, you are deliberately setting up yourself for delays.

Action Point: What is that goal that has been in your mind to do for some time now? Plan towards taking that bold step to start it. For example if it's learning a new language and it will cost you money, set some cash aside daily and plan to do it next week or in few days, call that tutor or language school and start to learn that language skill. With that, you have overcome the procrastinating spirit that doesn't want you to learn that skill.

If it's taking some classes in a particular field, for example music classes. Call the music school and ask them what they require from schedule to pricing and till the starting day, get the required information and without putting it till another day, ask for the starting day, pay and start. Is it learning a new language, this will open doors for you for more job opportunities and ability to reach out to people the more e.g. People who speak Spanish. Learning a musical skill will train you the more in what it takes to sing well and who knows, after taking the music classes. You might be selected to partake in a musical competition for having a trained voice. Then, you start to go places. Darling, do not short change you by postponing the learning of that skill.

Envision yourself
achieving your dream.

Envisioning means seeing. It means seeing yourself achieving your dream. See yourself achieving that goal with your inner eye; it makes the process faster because the more you are picturing the end goal, the more the zeal and effort that unconsciously comes on you to finish that assignment. As you see yourself writing that book, see the finished copy of the book, see yourself even doing a book launch on the book, with that in mind, unconsciously, things will get itself done through you. Learn to picture learn to use your mind's eye, your inner eye, learn to imagine and very soon I tell you, you shall see the physical manifestation. In Genesis 15:5-6 "And he brought him forth abroad, and said, Look now towards heaven, and tell the stars, if thou be able to number them: and he said unto him, So shall thy seed be. And he believed in the Lord ; and he counted it for him for righteousness.

From the above Scripture, we can see the power of looking which could be called envisioning. The Lord had to tell Abraham to look at the stars, so that he could start picturing his seeds as numerous as the stars and it became so.

Action point: For example, if you want to slim down or loose some fat, take a picture of your former self of the weight you want to reduce to and begin seeing yourself that way, soon, you will become so. See yourself on that campus doing graduation and encourage yourself by going to graduation ceremonies.

Focus on your goal.

Focusing on your goal according to the Merriam-Webster dictionary means to direct your attention or effort at one goal. To concentrate on a particular specific area or goal. To focus your energy, thoughts and mind on one thing. If you do this, you will finish quickly and feel more accomplished. For example, having 3 or 4 areas of concentration then not succeeding in it is worse than having one or two areas of concentration and then finish quickly and then feel a sense of accomplishment. ONE THING AT A TIME PLS. A wonderful man of God says that the only reason why men fail is Broken Focus! Focus!!Focus!!!.

Action Point: Settle down or sit and write all you desire to do according to the order of priority that you want them. Pick one or two of those desires and put all your zeal, energy, and mind. By the time you finish one, you will feel a sense of accomplishment in that area and will experience the joy of completion.

Giving up is not an option

To give up means to quit something you started. You see some people start an project and stop. It is not a good idea to be quitting what you started. Don't quit that project, that program, that schooling, that goal that you started. The Bible says in Matthew 24:13 "He that endure to the end shall be saved".

Action Point: Look at any goal you started and could not finish, set to go and complete it right now. Its all about ending it. There is no joy in starting a goal and stopping it on the way, it brings unfulfillment and lack of satisfaction. Go back and finish that which you started.

Have faith or belief in the Lord

Having Faith or belief in God means knowing, trusting or relying on the Lord and his power. It will be awesome if everyone can understand that we did not create ourselves but that we were all created by God. Pls, learn to understand that you were created and moulded and formed by the Lord God Almighty. You did not not form or create yourself. Thus you should always show your reliance by asking or praying to that God for directions in all your steps. Provers3:6 KJV In all thy ways acknowledge him, and he shall direct thy paths.

Action Point: Whatever you decide to pursue as an individual, pray put it in the hands of the Lord and go after getting it done, and it will be done. If there is no pain, there is no gain.

If there is no pain, there is no gain.

Some people want to achieve great success in life without putting or investing effort. You see, God blesses efforts. The Bible says in Gal. 6:7 "Be not deceived; God is not mocked, for whatsoever a man sow, that shall he also reap". If you invest little effort in a goal, you will get little result, likewise, if you invest great effort in achieving something, you will get great result.

Sow effort into that goal and it will yield result. The investment that you put into that goal is what you will achieve back. Invest time into your prayer and bible reading aspect, input more of your effort on that project, invest in that friendship, relationship or marriage. Invest also in knowing your vocation or job, bring in new points and ideas. The Bible also says in Genesis 8:20-22 KJV "And Noah s long as the earth remains, seedtime and harvest will not cease. Put something down to get something from it. Don't lazy around.

Action Point: Look at any area of your life that needs improvement and decide to put more effort. For example, do you think you talk too much, take your Bible and concordance, open the Bible to the "sparing your words" page, write the verse and place it is in the Bible, gather more of those scriptures on words, meditate and ponder over it, see it, say it, pray it into your life, do this consistently daily for like a month, firstly you will get used to sowing spiritual truths into your life and secondly, youwill see results and will be talking less because of the fact that you are using spiritual truths to help that spiritual area in your life. This happened to me at a point I was dealing with an area in my life, I had to get my Bible and search for scriptures on words, meditated on them, and God so good, it worked for me. It also applies to your family and human relationships, is there someone in your life that you think is very important to you e:g your significant other(your partner),sibling, parent, close friend. Pick up your phone and call him or her, send an e-mail, write a note, drop a card/message or token and express yourself to them one by one, this boosts and increases self fulfillment. Be at peace with yourself and your relationships. Statistics prove that people who give and receive love are more healthy and recover quickly from illnesses than those who don't, because it helps them stabilize emotionally, thus solidifying their overall welfare.

Lastly, concerning your vocation or academic or job, put in more of your effort, be creative in that area, if you are a student, study more and do researches in areas that you need to know more. If you are a machinist, do more research on areas that could get you informed about other machines. If you are into the health field, you have to be up and doing, learn and be open to new ideas in the health field e.g researches about what could possibly get rid of HIV, Ebola and all STD's. Likewise an engineer needs to be aware of new development and aspects in the engineering sector and a computer Engineer needs to put more into knowing the advance software and hardware to ease technological advancement.

Just keep moving yourself forward.

Do everything you can to keep moving yourself forward. Do something progressive. Take a certification course. Upgrade your skills either vocational or home skill, or feminine related like cooking skills or masculine related like Barbing skills. It could be taking a writing class or decorating or makeup class or Plumbing classes. Sharpen that talent of yours that you or others have observed. You are born to be dynamic and you are a dynamic being. Keep keeping on. Let no situation stop you. Do something daily to move yourself forward. Don't stop learning and improving yourself. I read a newspaper page about a 97 year old who just graduated high school. Probably he did not realize to do it at his younger age and when he realized at 97years, he decided to achieve that goal of moving forward which he did. Darling, Its not too late to keep moving forward. I have seen graduates of college at 50 years /55 years of age. My old man went back to college at a later age and it was very exemplary to the children. It inspired me personally that if he can do it at that age, then the sky is not even my limit.

Action steps: Decide to progress in any aspect you think you want or need to and do it. You could take affordable online classes or search for individual that could render professional training at affordable rates. It could be skills to help your spiritual life like counseling, skills to help your relationships like communication or skills to help you at the home front like cooking, decorating, baking, cleaning, makeup or hairstyling, nail design art, headgear or wrapper tying, barbing, plumbing, electricity. Don't stop learning. Sweetheart, exercise your mind.

K- Keep Benefitting Associations.

Who are the people that you walk or associate with. This is worth reflecting on. Statistics has shown that human beings are easily influenced. If you are always with someone that is furious when angered, sooner or later, you will become furious when angered. If you associate with thieves and evil gangsters, no matter how innocent you are, sooner or later, you will be stealing too. The Bible says in Proverbs. "He that walketh with the wise shall be wise. Associate with people who are well behaved and have good conduct, people who have good character, people who are wise, trustworthy and intelligent, sooner or later, you will find your self being like that. Do not move with mediocre or idiots. Association tend to have a great impact on everyone, this is because we carry a little bit of each other around, we rub on each other either consciously or unconsciously. Darling, watch your association. It will go a long way and take you a long way.

Action Points: Take out some 30 minutes out of your time, either in the evening or in the morning and reflect on all your association (friends). Determine in your heart to get rid of the bad or non-benefitting ones and choose the ones that are moving you forward or you are moving them forward and watch your life change thereafter. Ask yourself questions like "What am I gaining from this association that can move me forward". If peradventure you are gaining something from that association, then keep that association or friend, if there is nothing you are gaining, end the association right away.

Learn to Love yourself.

Loving yourself means that you enjoy and really like your entire being. You value and like who you are. You like your personality, your stature, your body and your totality. You don't prioritize others at your one expense. You know your worth and you value it. You appreciate yourself and you take care of your self. It even increases your self esteem and confidence if you love yourself. It is important to note that it might become very difficult for you to love someone else, if at first you do not love yourself.

Action Point: Look at yourself in the mirror and give yourself a kiss, appreciate and admire all your body parts, the shape of your mouth, the shape of your nose, the shape of your ear, admire your stature, kiss and admire your own self in the mirror. Tell yourself that "I am elegant and attractive". "I am intelligent and beautiful, I am beauty and brainy if you are a woman. Affirm and raise your head up high if you are a male that I am handsome, I am loveable, I am efficient, I am effective, I am a love child of a love God. Proclaim good statements to yourself saying I am a quality human being, kind, compassionate and loving. It is of importance to know that once you say it out, it connects with your minds and sends information to you body to produce that kind of behavior you want your body to be like. Learn to love yourself.

Make good choices.

Just as there are two sides to a coin, there are two sides to life-the good and the bad. When we make good choices, we progress and are positively impacted and when we make bad choices, we are negatively impacted. I heard someone say that there are two types of pain in life-the pain of discipline and the pain of regret. When you go through the pain of discipline, you achieve something worthwhile, you are proud of yourself. When you experience the pain of regret, you regret over something that you should have done but did not. The Bible says in Joshua 24:15 "And if it seem evil unto you to serve the Lord, choose you this day whom you will serve ;whether the gods which your fathers served that were on the other side of the flood, or the gods of the Amorites in whose land ye dwell: but as for me and my house, we will serve the Lord."

You can see from the above verse where Joshua declared openly whom he will serve. That is the power of good choices at work.

Action Points: Make good choices by looking at your options critically and prayerfully and choose the right ones.

Never forget to Plan ahead.

Never making plans or forgetting to plan ahead are steps that will keep you from getting ahead in life. Think about your tomorrow, think about your next 2 days, next three days and so on. Think about your next week, next two weeks, next three weeks, and so on and so forth. Also, think about your next month, your next two months, your next three months and on and on and on. Think about your next year. Practice thinking ahead and planning ahead of time. It means putting into consideration what you want to achieve tomorrow.

Action point: In a quiet place, take a sheet of paper, think about what you want to achieve tomorrow, write it down with dates and deadline and set to work on it. Learn to anticipate needs.

Organize your life

Its means putting values and things in their place. According to world-renowned beauty products founder, Mary Kay Ash, she says that she personally organizes her main values in life by Putting Faith (or God) first, Family Second and Career as the last. So remember, the next time, you are stuck in choosing either of the two, remember to choose according to this standard. It works.

Action Point: Learn to Prioritize by putting Faith first, Family or children second and lastly career last.

Also, learn to put your items and things where they belong, do not live a scattered life, arrange, set, organize according to color, size, materials and so on

Preparing well pays off.

Whatever it is you want to do. Learn to prepare for it. Don't just jump into doing it. Prepare, be ready, it gets you composed, it makes you get on track. Don't rush into doing an examination, read, study, get the necessary materials. Is it for an interview, project or examination. Do not believe in firebrigade approach. A firebrigade approach makes you to read for an examination a night before having it instead of preparing weeks or days ahead. To reach your goal in life, learn to put adequate preparation into that which you want to do. It sets you on and gets you ready, it makes you more confident. There is a kind of confident feeling that comes on one who is well prepared for an event. For example, if you want to make a presentation or examination, you have to get ready, practice, prepare, study or read the necessary piece to make you come out bright and I tell you, before that day, you will be confident, ready and prepared for the presentation or examination. It is well worth it.

Action Point: Is there a project or examination you are preparing for, read, study, get prepared, get the past questions that they might ask you there, revise and practice repeatedly before someone. I tell you that you will be surprised at the confident feeling that you will feel afterwards. Do you have a plan to go somewhere in the future, plan and start preparing for it. Prepare, Prepare, Prepare.

Quash all timewasters.

Time is the measurement by which we live. It is very important. It is a measure of how far we have gone in life. Don't waste it. Guard it, redeem it. The Bible says redeeming the time because the days are evil. Wake up, show up, spend your time well. Don't be a sluggard or sluggish person. Be time- conscious. Remove excesses that could act as a time wasters from your way. Play, but don't overplay, be productive with your phone calls and receiving, don't be excessive. Some people waste time, they are in all gathering, all events, all ceremonies. Remember the Holy Book in Proverbs 21:17 which says that _____ "He that loves pleasure shall never be rich. Pleasure wastes the time you could use to do productive assignments. In some countries, you see adults playing traditional games early in the morning, don't they think. Anything that wastes time, be it talking or gossiping on phone, unnecessary, videocalling or chatting, oversleeping should be stopped.

Action Points: Sit down and look at your next 24 hours, gazette what you want to use each hours for. There are 168 hrs in a week, plan how you want to use these 168 hrs. If you are a morning person, plan to do your most job in the morning, likewise, if you are a night person. Plan to do your most job at night.

Read and Study, no matter what.

The place of reading cannot be overemphasized.

Read books, journals, articles ranging form sports to money, health, animals, marriage, religion and politics. Get informed, knowledge is power, an uninformed man is a deformed man. You cannot grow above what you know. Remember the Holy Bible in 2 Timothy 2:15 "Study to shew thyself approved unto God, a workman that need not to be ashamed, rightly dividing the word of truth."

"My people perish because of lack of knowledge. You can only be deceived by what you do not know. You cannot be deceived by what you know. Read and Study. I know an exerpt that says Reading skims the surface in a book, but when you study, you dig deep, it makes you discover the treasure. When you study, you dig deep, the Bible says in _____" Study to show yourself approved unto God, a workman that needed not to be ashamed, rightly dividing the word of truth.

Action Point: When you study a particular topic, you get insight because you delve, think, meditate, compare and ponder on it and thus you receive insights. Pick a book, either secular or nonsecular and decide to read it through and even Study it. Then you will see how much you have gained from it.

Stay motivated.

To be motivated means to have the willingness, ability or enablement to do something. When you are motivated to read, you want to read. Stay motivated, don't lose your motivation, do things or act. Stay on top of your life game. Be encouraged. Don't get discouraged with life. Whatever you know that inspires or motivates you, be it songs, a piece of art or a piece of writing or people, stay around them. Sometime ago I lost my job and almost got discouraged, that was when I read an excerpt that says "Know your calling". That was how I discerned the writing gifts that God placed inside of me. To encourage myself and others thus giving birth to this book. Don't let little things discourage you. Be strong, don't be discouraged. You are on top of that situation. You are a positive being, you are not a negative being. The things happening are to prove and develop you. Don't because of one little situation put your head down Sweetheart.

Action Point: Is there any area of life that wants to get you discouraged. Pull yourself together and get yourself inspired and motivated using that which inspires you, that song, that writing, that art piece. Stay motivated and don't get discouraged.

THINK BIG.

Think large. Enlarge your thinking. Do not limit yourself. Think of yourself doing big things. Don't be a small thinker. It is well with your soul. You've got all it takes sweetheart.

Action point: Don't say I want little things. Dream and see yourself doing big and large things and it shall soon be so.

Ultimately, YOU are the determinant of your future.

Nobody determines your future for you. It is you that decides it. Your way of life and your habits go a long way. What do you do most of the time. Are you someone who likes pleasure? Always playing jesting, hanging around.

Are you someone that wastes your resources, time, money and possessions, remember that we are stewards of these things. If you are diligent and hardworking in your business, you will stand before kings and not before mean men. The Holy Book says in _____Seest thou a man that is diligent in his business, he will not stand before mean men, he will stand before kings. If you are diligent in your field or in your business, you will come out well and be known for excellence and you will secure a future for yourself. If you are not hardworking but lazy, always lying around like a sluggard, then I am scared that your future might be good. The Holy Book says that _____Like a door easily opens on its hinges so does a lazy man on his bed". It could take some, sweating, labour, focus, night vigils and a little extra effort but whatever goals you set before God and yourself, you will get it.

Action Point: What is that you want to be in the future. You will determine it by setting and resetting that goal, keeping at it, trying and trying again without relenting and my dear, you will come through as an achiever.

Verbal out what want to become.

Speak it, affirm often, that which you want to be. You see, the power of word cannot be overemphasized. Talk it, say it, express it out verbally. The talking (shouting) team is the winning team. By saying it, you are overcoming defeat, you are possessing your possession. Say it out loud. There is power in the words of your mouth. The Holy Book says that "Death and life are in the power of the tongue and those that love it will eat the fruit there of. Darling, learn to say, learn to speak, learn to declare. They can take you to places. Gen 1:3 says" And God said, "Let there be light and there was light". Dear firend, there is much power in the tongue. Declare it and say it how you want it to be. You will see that your circumstances will soon line up with your words.

Action Point: Get a blank sheet of paper and write out how God- given dream. State it clearly. Open your bible to scripture that supports your dreams, Say it, speak, it using the word of God. It is powerful. The Holy book says that it is sharper than two edged –sword_____. For instace, when I was having an ailment, I saw myself being healed of that ailment. I picked up my Bible, turned to 1Peter 2:27 "Who his own self bore my sins in his own body upon a tree so that I being dead to sin may live unto righteousness and by whose stripes I am healed. Say this aloud over and over again believing it. If you are experiencing lack, go to Philippian 4:19 and say that "My God shall supply all my needs according to his riches in glory by Christ Jesus. If you have the fear of death, go to the verse of the Bible that says that I shall not die but live to declare the works of the Lord in the land of the living. Declare it, say it out, speak and believe God over your situation.

Wisdom is a virtue you should possess.

Wisdom means the application of knowledge. It is a virtue one should possess. Be wise in all the phase of your, its very important. Be wise spiritiually (Spiritual wisdom). Be wise in your relationships, even in your home or marriage. Be wise in your profession or vocation. The Bible says wisdom is the principle things, get wisdom, and in all thy getting, get understanding.

Action Point: If you desire more wisdom from our Lord, learn to read one chapter from the Book of proverbs daily. Some wise folks has determined that since the Book of Proverbs has 31 chapters in its entirety and there are averagely 31 days in a most, then, it will do a lot of benefit to one to read one chapter for each day accordingly. It is loaded with so many insights from King Solomon who was the wisest man who ever lived.

Xamine Yourself often

To examine means to weigh, look at, observe a dn look very attentively to your life situations. Learn to ask yourself questions. Judge yourself. The holy book says that _____ if you judge yourself, you will not be judged. Examine yourself to know the areas you need to develop or build, and do this from time to time. Look at your weaknesses and work on them, look at your strength and encourage yourself. It will energize your spirit. It will make you see yourself.

Action Point: Take yourself to a solitary place, using a blank sheet of paper, write your strengths on one side, write your weaknesses on the other side. Pray. Ask the Lord to help you in the areas of your weaknesses. Note it and using corresponding scriptures and spiritual mediation, develop those areas. If you need grace in a particular area, open the bible to that area, and meditate or ponder over it. This is how to grow spiritually.

You are the one that determines your own luck.

Some people believe that others are luckier than them. The truth is that champions pay the price of whatsoever they become or achieve. Champions dream and go after it for actualization. They set goals and aim to achieve them, which is the main aim of this book. They believe in themselves that they will succeed in whatever they set their mind or soul to achieve. They are not lazy, thus people see them as lucky, because they make things happen by setting their minds to a goal and going ahead to achieve it. That is their secret.

Action Point: If you want to become a champion. First write your goal down and work at achieving it. Don't be lazy about it. Pursue it with zeal.

Zeal is important

Zeal is dedication or enthusiasm for something you are pursuing. If you have zeal, you are willing, energized and motivated. It is passion, fervor, being on fire, eagerness, enthusiasm, vigour, appetite, energy and intensity.

Action Point: Endeavour to put the above (zeal) into anything you want to do.

Printed in the United States
By Bookmasters